Dedication

For Brittney, Geoff and Veronica,
who grew up with Ali.

To my husband and best friend, Rick, whose
skills at listening and supporting me through
the lifetime development of this book –
I couldn't have done it without you.

To Rod and Greg,
who always believed in Ali.

In memory of my loving parents,
Paul and Barbara.

Psalm 37:4–5

Use the QR code to visit my *website* for more activities

Ali's Big Adventure

Copyright © 2024 by Roxie Fiste. All rights reserved.

All rights reserved. No part of this publication may be reproduced, distributed or transmitted in any form or by any means, including photocopying, recording, or other electronic or mechanical methods, without the prior written permission of the publisher, except in the case of brief quotations embodied in critical reviews and certain other noncommercial uses permitted by copyright law.

Although the author and publisher have made every effort to ensure that the information in this book was correct at press time, the author and publisher do not assume and hereby disclaim any liability to any party for any loss, damage, or disruption caused by errors or omissions, whether such errors or omissions result from negligence, accident, or any other cause.

Adherence to all applicable laws and regulations, including international, federal, state and local governing professional licensing, business practices, advertising, and all other aspects of doing business in the US, Canada or any other jurisdiction is the sole responsibility of the reader and consumer.

Neither the author nor the publisher assumes any responsibility or liability whatsoever on behalf of the consumer or reader of this material. Any perceived slight of any individual or organization is purely unintentional.

The resources in this book are provided for informational purposes only and should not be used to replace the specialized training and professional judgment of a health care or mental health care professional.

Neither the author nor the publisher can be held responsible for the use of the information provided within this book. Please always consult a trained professional before making any decision regarding treatment of yourself or others.

ISBN: 979-8-89109-574-8 (Paperback)
ISBN: 979-8-89109-576-2 (Hardcover)
ISBN: 979-8-89109-575-5 (Ebook)

SunPony Press

ALI'S
BIG ADVENTURE!

ROXIE FISTE

Ali is a Puffball. Puffballs are soft, rubbery creatures that live in a hidden valley near the Southern Cliffs. They like to bounce!

One day Ali tried to catch a dragonfly. His parents told him many times, "Don't bounce alone. You're too little to control your bounce!" But, today, Ali forgot.

When Ali came to a stop, he looked around for a path home.
He quickly discovered he was lost!
Ali sat down to think.
But he was so tired from bouncing, he fell *asleep*.

"Hello," a voice said, surprising the puffball.

"Hello," Ali answered, timidly blinking at the human.

'I'm Mika!" the youth said as he sat down beside the puffball.

'I'm Ali," the puffball sighed heavily.

'How did you get here, Ali?" Mika asked.

Mika had heard stories about puffballs from his tribe.

He had seen drawings of them. His family had told him where they thought puffballs lived, but he was very surprised to meet one!

Ali began to wail...

'I tried to catch a dragonfly and bounced away from home – Now I'm Lost!!"

Big tears ran down his face.

"Don't worry." Mika patted Ali's soft, yellow head. "I'll help you! It's a long walk to your home and it's late! Are you hungry?"

Ali nodded, his tummy rumbling.

Mika led Ali to a small cave he liked to camp in.
"I'll take you home in the morning,"
Mika said as they ate.
His tummy full, Ali *fell asleep* listening to tree frogs.
They reminded him of home.

The next day, Ali and Mika headed toward the puffball's home. A short time later they met a golden pony eating clover. Mika introduced himself and Ali.

"Hmmm, I'm Scout!" the pony said.

"I'm taking Ali to his home near the Southern Cliffs. Would you like to come with us?" Mika asked.

"Hmmm, climb on my back and I'll carry you both there!" Scout boasted!

Scout swiftly carried Ali and Mika out of the forest.

Soon they entered the Valley of the Sun.

Everything was hot!

"We're not far from the Sand Palace," Mika urged.

"We can be there by lunch!"

Scout sped up – He was hungry!

Scout carried Ali and Mika to the Sand Palace gate where they met a *watchman.*

"My name is Gareth."
His deep, rumbly voice made Ali giggle.

He led them to a room for their lunch.
He even had fresh hay and water for Scout!

After the friends had eaten, Gareth came with some balloons that floated above his head. He handed them to Mika.

"These will shade all of you from the sun," Gareth smiled.

"Thank you!" Mika took the magical balloons, quickly tying them around Scout's middle.

Saying goodbye to Gareth the friends headed off.

Scout carried Mika and Ali out of the Valley of the Sun and began to climb up the Southern Cliffs.

When Scout finally came to the top of the Southern Cliffs the friends came to a stop. The bridge on the path was broken!

Ali cried, "How will I ever get home now?"
"Don't worry, little buddy," said Mika. "I'll think of something!"
After pacing back and forth Mika got an idea! He quickly tied a balloon around Ali. He tied two more around himself.
"This will work! Come on, Ali – Come on Scout!"
With that Mika jumped over the edge of the cliff.
Scout followed with Ali.

Mika and Scout landed safely a couple minutes later and pulled off their balloons.

A short time later Ali landed.
Or almost landed!
When Ali dropped to the ground he began to bounce!
"OH, NO!" Mika cried, running after the puffball.
"Come on Scout! We have to catch Ali
before he gets lost again!"
When Mika got his arms around Ali, he tripped!

Ali shot out of his arms, bounced, then landed,

KER-SPLASH!

Right in the middle of a stream!

"Hmmm, that was some bounce!" exclaimed Scout.
"Look," Mika pointed across the stream.
Ali *squealed*, jumping out of the water.

"WELCOME HOME, Ali!"
They shOuted and ran to meet him!
Ali's parents rested their heads
against his, glad he was safe.
When Ali explained how Mika and Scout had
helped him, his family rushed to thank them.

Soon it was time for Mika and Scout to go. Ali *smiled* as his new friends started for home. He hoped he would see Mika and Scout again, someday.

The End

Create Your Own Character

www.ingramcontent.com/pod-product-compliance
Lightning Source LLC
LaVergne TN
LVHW070844250326
834741LV00011B/126